AROUND LONDON

Text by Daniela Celli
Illustrations by Laura Re

DEAR PARENTS

Nowadays there are a considerable amount of things to make life easier for those adults who decide to travel with children.
But do you want to know a secret?
Nothing is more effective than a good story!
British writer Rudyard Kipling used to do this to entertain his children during their long voyages by steamer to Africa, and so did James Matthew Barrie with the little Londoners of Kensington.
This book is meant to be a little help in turning a trip to London into an exciting experience for the whole family—a guide full of stories and games to play while traveling from your sofa or for real...
Among the pages of this guide, you will discover all the adventures that I experienced while exploring the fascinating British capital with my children, with additional, incredible curiosities and a pinch of *supercalifragilisticexpialidocious* that London gives to those who look at it through the eyes of fantasy and that I hope will reach you, too.

To BG,
my jazz to the route to Oz.

Daniela Celli

GOOD MORNING, KIDS. LET ME INTRODUCE MYSELF...

My name is SIR RAVEN, and it will be a real pleasure to take you around LONDON with me. I'm sure we'll have a lot of fun because this city is full of fascinating places and mysterious stories: Did you know, for example, that on Christmas Day a GHOST wanders through the rooms of Buckingham Palace? And that there is a huge *T. REX* waiting for you at the Natural History Museum?
Here is how we will be able to see everything: I have prepared FOUR ITINERARIES for you that will lead us to the discovery of fantastic places and characters.
Each itinerary begins with A MAP, where you will find the planned route along with some interesting facts.
Also, between one neighborhood and another I organized some GAMES to have fun together.

THAT'S ALL, MY FRIENDS! LET'S GO!

ITINERARIES

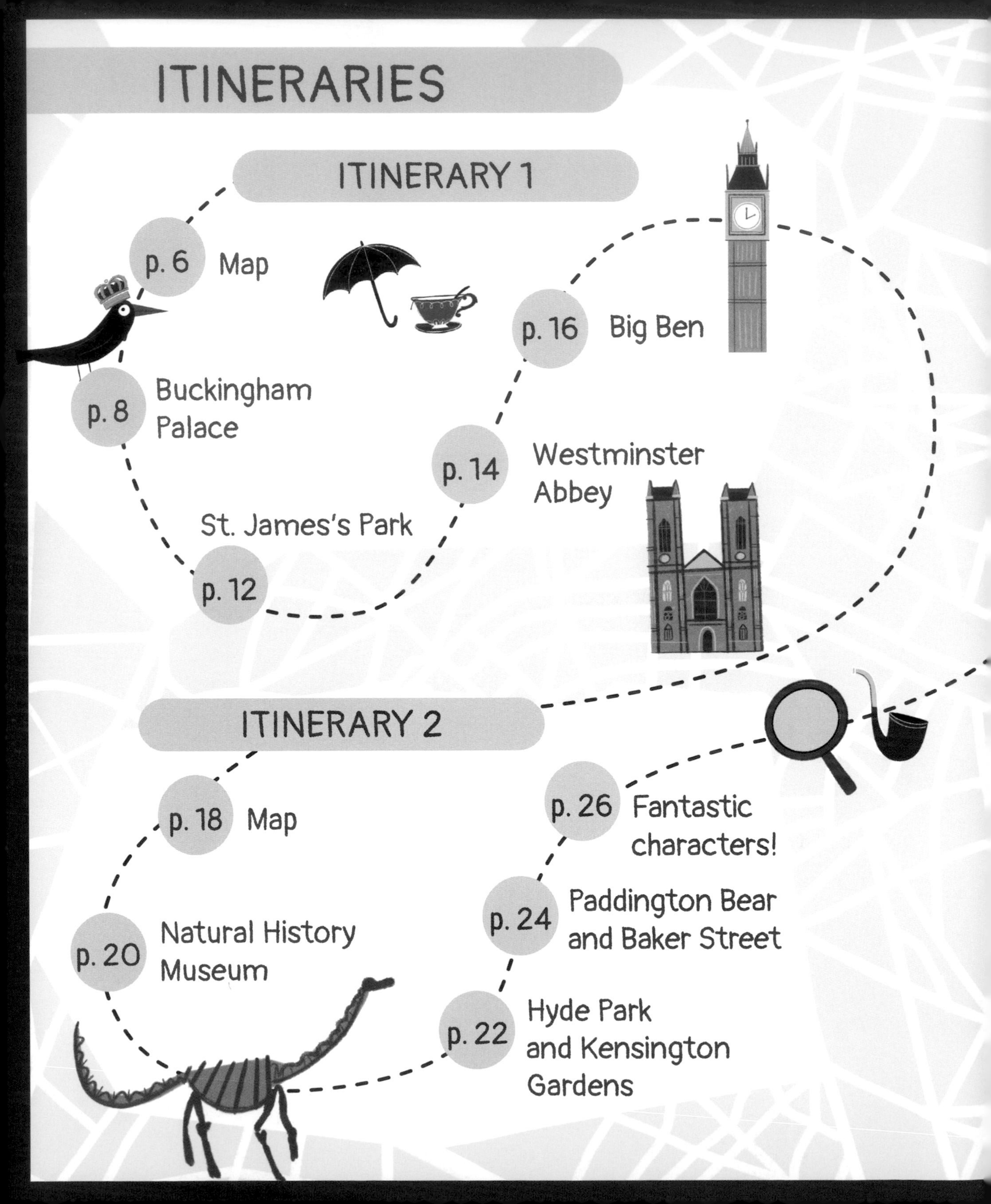

ITINERARY 1

ITINERARY 2

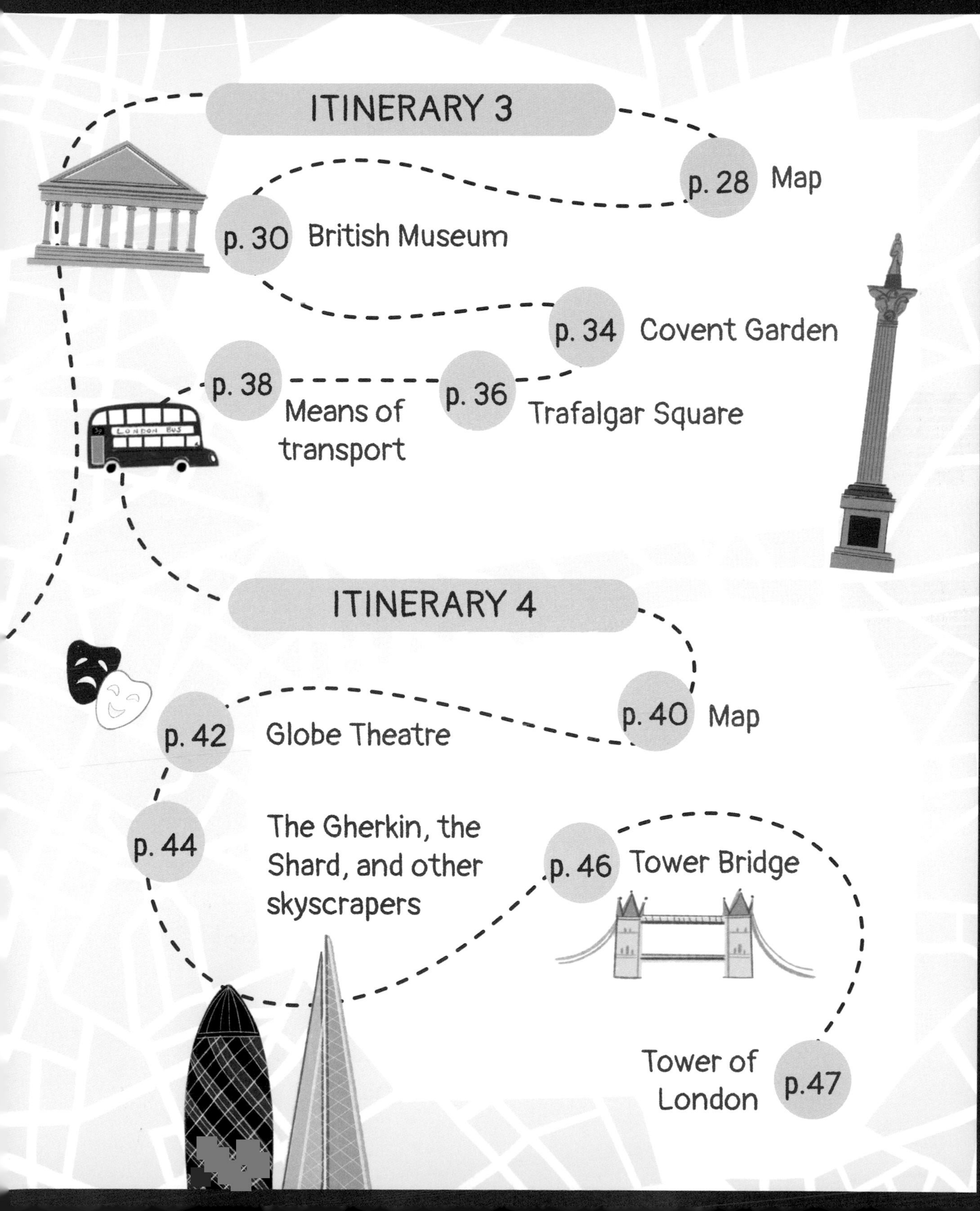
ITINERARY 3
p. 28 Map
p. 30 British Museum
p. 34 Covent Garden
p. 36 Trafalgar Square
p. 38 Means of transport
LONDON BUS
ITINERARY 4
p. 40 Map
p. 42 Globe Theatre
p. 44 The Gherkin, the Shard, and other skyscrapers
p. 46 Tower Bridge
p.47 Tower of London

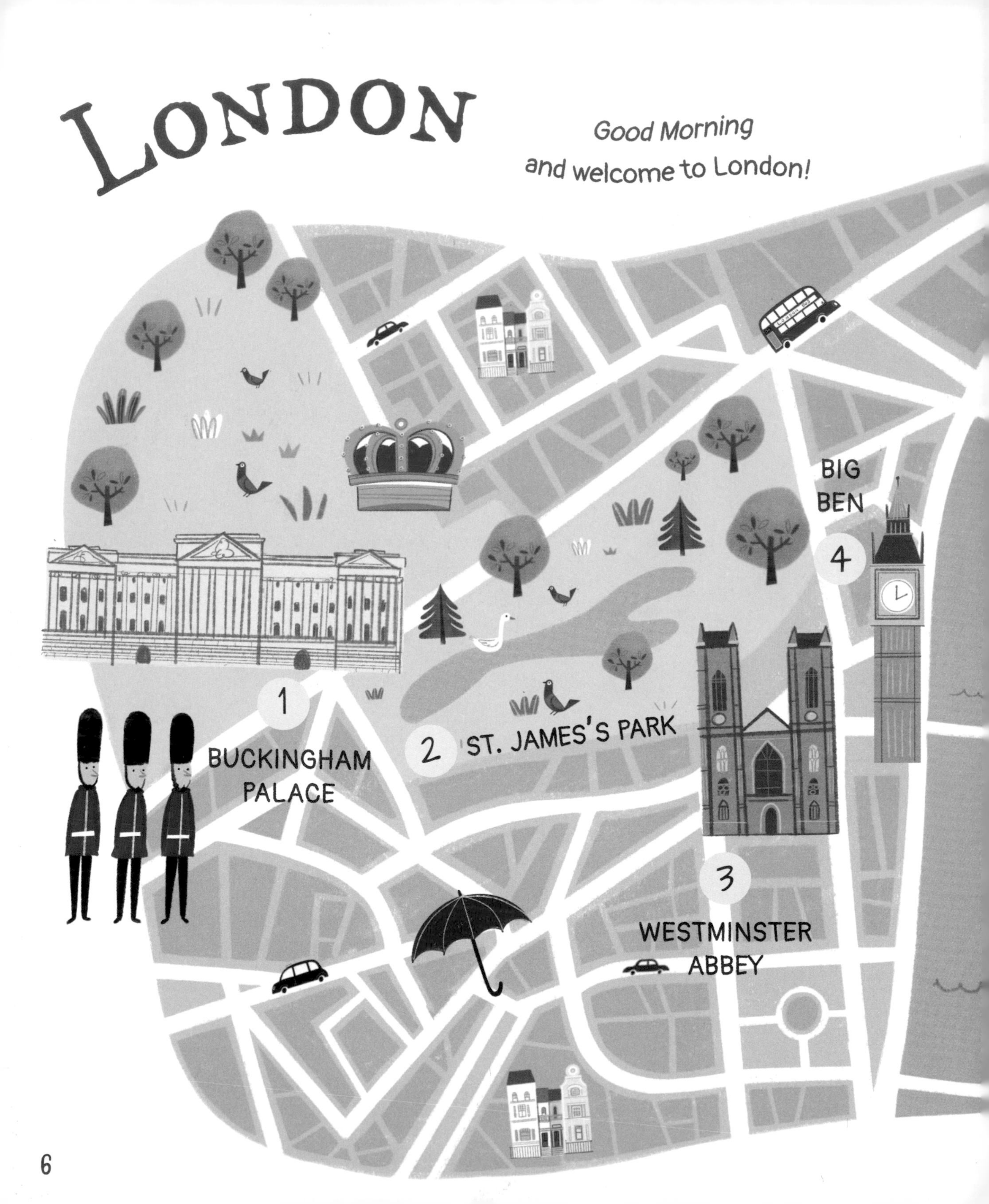
LONDON
Good Morning
and welcome to London!
BIG
BEN
4
1
BUCKINGHAM
PALACE
2 ST. JAMES'S PARK
3
WESTMINSTER
ABBEY

ITINERARY 1

Today we are going to discover the stories and curiosities of one of the most famous *BOROUGHS* of the British capital, the *City of Westminster*, a real city within a city! This large district is on the north bank of the Thames, where there is the King's Palace, surrounded by magnificent parks.

THIS IS WHERE OUR ADVENTURE BEGINS!

• To each their own

London is divided into *32 boroughs*, each one with its own name and coat of arms, which are sometimes decorated with animals or legendary figures, such as griffins and dragons. The symbol of *Westminster* is a shield held up by two lions!

• A gift for the spirits

London is cut in two by the *River Thames*, the second longest river in the UK.

It was once believed that it was inhabited by spirits and goblins, and Londoners used to offer them gifts by throwing objects of all kinds into the water. Some of these, such as the *Battersea Shield*, have been found and can be seen in the *British Museum*.

THAMES

UNDERGROUND

BUCKINGHAM PALACE

It is with great pleasure that I present to you the first leg of our journey! *Welcome to the palace*!

Buckingham Palace is the residence of the king of England, CHARLES III.

The palace has 775 rooms, including 52 rooms for guests, 188 rooms for the staff, and 78 bathrooms! The royal residence also includes a cinema, an indoor swimming pool, a doctor's office, a post office, and an ATM, plus much more!

The palace is surrounded by a park the size of 20 football fields, and among its wonders is a magnificent rose garden, a large lake, and even an islet where the court bees live, producing the honey used by the court chefs to garnish cakes and sweets for the royal family!

- **The Changing of the Guard**

In front of the gates of *Buckingham Palace* it is possible to witness the ceremony of the soldiers changing guard. The guards wear red coats and characteristic bear-fur hats. Do you know why the hats are so big? They made the soldiers look taller in battle!

DO YOU WANT TO KNOW THE SECRETS OF *BUCKINGHAM PALACE*?

• A ghostly guest

The land where *Buckingham Palace* stands today was once occupied by a monastery. Perhaps this is why on Christmas Day the ghost of a monk wanders the rooms of the palace rattling noisy chains.
EVERY YEAR THERE ARE THOSE WHO SWEAR THAT THEY HAVE SEEN IT: DO YOU BELIEVE IT?

• Moving lights

Until recently, cleaning the palace's huge chandeliers was a real undertaking. A whole army of workers had to dust thousands of crystal drops, climbing long, rickety stairs.

TODAY EVERYTHING IS SIMPLER. JUST PRESS A BUTTON ON A REMOTE CONTROL AND THE CHANDELIER DROPS TO HUMAN HEIGHT!

• Real time

There are over 600 clocks in the queen's residence! Twice a year, a team of clockmakers takes care of moving the hands forward or backward by an hour for daylight savings. Do you know how long it takes?
TWO FULL DAYS!

• No bell

Do you want to know if the queen is home? Just check which flag is flying over *Buckingham Palace*!
If the royal banner is there, then *King Charles* is in the palace, while when she's out, the *Union Jack* swings on the pole.
EASY, RIGHT?

WHICH OF THESE CURIOUS FACTS IS YOUR FAVORITE?

ST. JAMES'S PARK

Welcome to *St. James's Park*, London's oldest royal park!

In the past this area was a real swamp! Then in 1532 it was purchased by HENRY VIII, who had it reclaimed to make it worthy of a king. Century after century, the monarchs modified and embellished the park according to their taste. KING JAMES I, who had a soft spot for exotic animals, filled it with crocodiles, camels, and even an elephant!

Today the park is a magnificent green space, dotted with flower beds and inhabited by hundreds of squirrels!

There is also a lake, crossed by a bridge from which you can enjoy a spectacular view; there are two islets—*West Island* and *Duck Island*—and a small reserve with 17 bird species, including ducks, swans, and a vast colony of pelicans.

Search and find

King James's pets are back in the park! Do you remember what they are? Try to find them!

WESTMINSTER ABBEY

Come on, friends, the abbey is waiting for us!

Westminster is one of the most famous churches in the world and the most important English place of worship.This is where queens and kings are crowned, royal weddings celebrated, and famous historical figures buried.

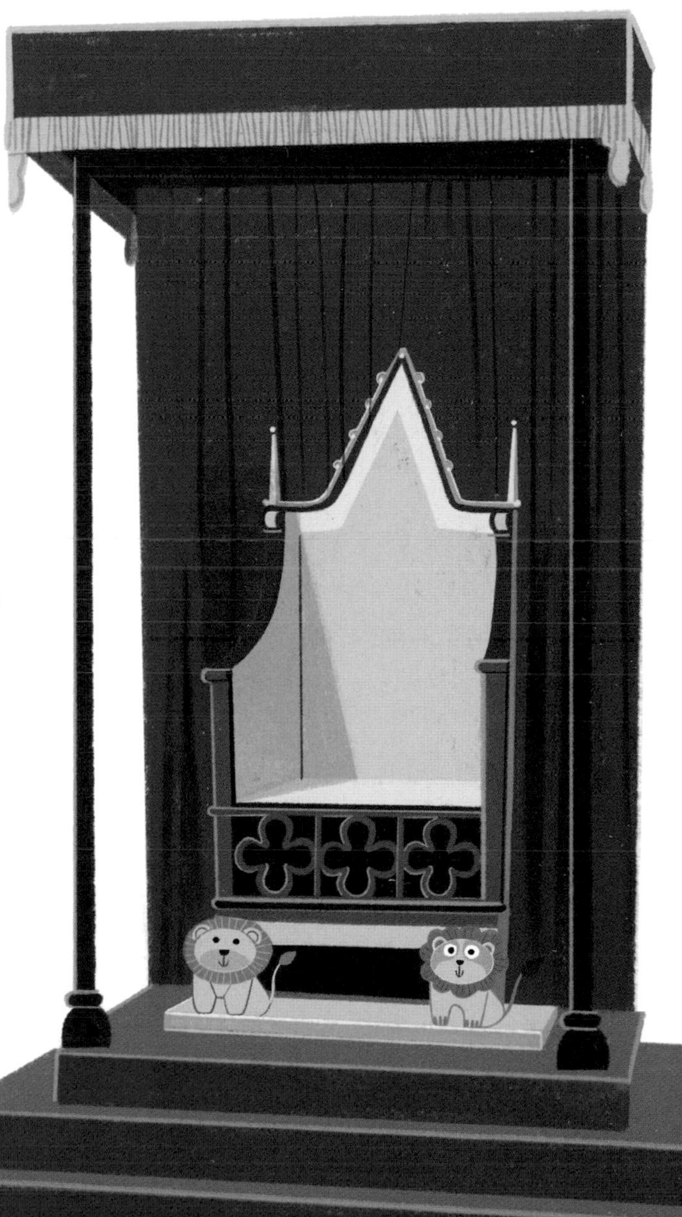

• A legendary theft

Under the seat of the *Coronation Chair,* the wooden throne on which English monarchs have been crowned for over 700 years, was a legendary stone, the *Stone of Scone.*

In 1950, four Scottish students managed to steal it, but while taking it, the stone slipped from the hands of one of them, breaking in half and fracturing two toes on his foot!

TODAY THE STONE HAS BEEN RESTORED AND IS SAFE IN EDINBURGH CASTLE.

Find the differences!

The legs of King Edward's throne are decorated with four gold lions.
Can you find the 6 differences between the two portraits in the image?

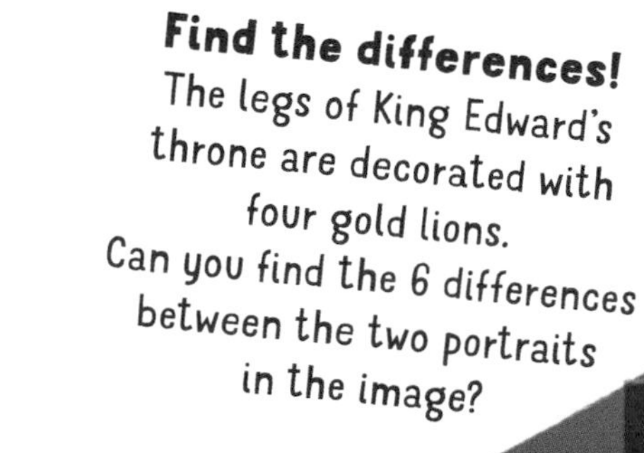

BIG BEN

Here is *Big Ben*!

Contrary to what everyone thinks, "*Big Ben*" is not the name of the clock tower of the Palace of *Westminster*, but rather of one of its five bells—the largest one.

Due to its exorbitant weight, equivalent to that of a *T. Rex* and a Triceratops combined, a sixteen-horse chariot was needed to transport it from the foundry to *Westminster*.

• A distinctive sound

The bells rang for the first time on May 31, 1859, but after only two months the *Great Bell* (as Big Ben is also called) broke.
A metal patch was used to repair it, and that is why today the bell has a very characteristic sound!

• A justified delay

Although a master clockmaker is in charge of checking that the tower clock strikes the correct time, over the years some unpredictable events have caused delays.

IN 1944, FOR EXAMPLE, A FLOCK OF BIRDS MOVED THE MINUTE HAND A FEW MILLIMETERS. I SWEAR TO YOU, I HAD NOTHING TO DO WITH IT!

• Flying over London

Let's take a look at the city from above?
Just cross the bridge and get on the *London Eye*, one of the tallest observation wheels in the world!

Are you ready for a new adventure?

ITINERARY 2

Today's journey begins in the beautiful *Kensington* neighborhood, where we will explore one of the most famous natural museums in the world. After the visit we will have tea in the park, and last, we will discover places dedicated to some fantastic characters! Are you curious to know who they are? Then *let's go*!

THAMES

- **The Rotten Row**

Alongside *Hyde Park* runs a quiet sandy path called *Rotten Row* (originally named the King's Road). Why such an unusual name? Long ago, this street was the den of dangerous criminals who waited for nighttime to attack passers-by.

In 1690, King William III ordered the installation of 300 lights, which transformed the road into the first lit street in England.

- **Explosive birthdays**

In London it is traditional to celebrate special occasions, such as royal birthdays, by firing blanks from a cannon. There are usually 21 "blows," but in *Hyde Park* an extra 20 shots are fired!

NATURAL HISTORY MUSEUM

Let's explore the museum!

The Natural History Museum houses one of the largest natural history collections in the world. Spread over four floors, there are over 70 million artifacts—from poisonous spiders to scary marine reptiles! A large section is dedicated to dinosaurs; here, in the midst of fascinating prehistoric skeletons, is a GIGANTIC *T. REX*!

• **What you need for a real adventure!**
To make your visit to the museum even more fun, you can pick up your explorer's backpack at the information desk. In addition to a very useful guide, you will find a safari hat and binoculars!

• ***Diplodocus***

For over a century, the reconstruction of a gigantic *DIPLODOCUS* has been one of the museum's most popular attractions. When not traveling around the UK, this giant long-necked sauropod dominates the entrance hall.

P Y I D

DO YOU WANT TO KNOW ITS NAME? LOOK FOR THE HIDDEN LETTERS AND PUT THEM IN THE RIGHT PLACE!

HYDE PARK AND KENSINGTON GARDENS

Although officially having different names, the two *royal parks* appear as one park the size of 350 football fields!

Hyde Park is the largest royal park in London. It is divided in two by a snake-shaped lake on which, in 1814, an incredible naval battle was staged, complete with galleons and fireworks! Imagine the show! Today, *Serpentine Lake* is an idyllic place where you can rent a rowboat and even swim.

- ***Peter Pan Cup***

A crazy swimming competition takes place in Hyde Park on Christmas Day. In a party atmosphere, participants, mostly brave people over 60 years old, challenge each other to swim 100 yards (91 meters) in the freezing waters of the lake.

A REAL TRIBUTE TO PETER PAN, THE CHILD WHO DID NOT WANT TO GROW UP!

Kensington Gardens were once the private gardens of *Kensington Palace*, home to royalty for over 300 years. Today they enchant visitors with tree-lined avenues, flowers, and numerous statues, including the one most loved by children: Peter Pan!

• **But now, how about *afternoon tea*?**
In the *Kensington Palace Orangery* you can enjoy a fabulous afternoon tea, a true tradition here in England! Along with a teapot you will be served cakes, treats to fill with cream and jam, and even savory sandwiches.

Search and find
Several cute green parrots live in Kensington Gardens. CAN YOU FIND ALL EIGHT?

PADDINGTON BEAR STATUE

Welcome to *Paddington Station!*

No, my friends, we are not here to take the train, but to see one of the most adorable sculptures in London: *Paddington Bear*!
To find it we have to go to platform 1, exactly where the *Brown family* finds the bear, in the film based on the book.

• Who is *Paddington Bear*?
Paddington is the famous character created by MICHAEL BOND in 1958. The writer came up with the idea after seeing a teddy bear in a shop near the station.

• Let's get to know Paddington Bear better:
1 He comes all the way from Peru.
2 Loves orange marmalade.
3 Always keeps an emergency sandwich under his hat.
4 Often gets into trouble!
5 Stays with the Brown family at their home at no. 32 Windsor Garden.

SHERLOCK HOLMES MUSEUM

Curious about what we're doing on *Baker Street?*

It is on this street, at number 221B, that famous British writer ARTHUR CONAN DOYLE imagined his most famous character: *Sherlock Holmes*!

Today, at this address, there is an interesting museum dedicated to the brilliant *detective*, and, further on, near the subway exit, stands his statue, in which he is portrayed with his unmistakable raincoat, hat, and pipe.

• **Let's get to know Sherlock Holmes better:**

1 He has remarkable deductive skills.
2 Loves impossible cases.
3 Is a wizard of disguises.
4 Plays the violin and smokes a pipe.
5 Has a faithful assistant, *Dr. Watson.*

FANTASTIC CHARACTERS

"Supercalifragilisticexpialidocious, even though the sound of it..."
Oh, how I love singing songs from *Mary Poppins* while flying over the rooftops of London!

• A very special nanny
Who can resist a nanny who, with one leap, takes you inside a painting and has a bag from which anything can come out, even a chandelier?

The film *Mary Poppins*, inspired by PAMELA LYNDON TRAVERS'S book, was released in 1964 and has continued to be loved by adults and children ever since.

The story takes place in London, and if you take a stroll between Big Ben and Kensington, you might recognize many locations from the film.

• The child who did not want to grow up

Everyone knows Peter Pan, the young boy who can fly and lives with the Lost Boys in Neverland.
But did you know that it was JAMES MATTHEW BARRIE WHO WROTE ABOUT HIS ADVENTURES?

One day while he was in Kensington Gardens, Barrie met a family with five children, who inspired him to write the adventures of the boy who does not want to grow up!

• The most famous young wizard in the world

Harry Potter, the famous protagonist of the series of books written by J. K. ROWLING, is an orphan raised by his horribly mean aunt and uncle. But on the night of his eleventh birthday, he receives an invitation to attend HOGWARTS SCHOOL OF WITCHCRAFT and WIZARDRY.

DO YOU KNOW WHERE THE TRAIN THAT REACHES THE SCHOOL DEPARTS FROM? FROM KING'S CROSS STATION, LONDON! IF YOU GO THERE, LOOK FOR PLATFORM 9¾: YOU MIGHT FIND HEDWIG THE OWL WAITING FOR YOU!

Another day around London!
1
BRITISH MUSEUM
UNDERGROUND
UNDERGROUND
2
COVENT
GARDEN
TRAFALGAR
SQUARE
3
UNDERGROUND

ITINERARY 3

Today we will start our visit from the heart of the district of *Bloomsbury*, where the extraordinary *British Museum* is located! Each section is dedicated to a different place and historical period, so visiting it will be like taking a trip back in time. And then let's see...what else is on the map? Point to the other stops.

THAMES

- **Smelly street lamps**
Before the invention of electricity, London was lit by gas lamps, some of which, like the one still present on Carting Lane, used gas from the sewers. Because of that, the smell in the area was terrible—so much so that the street was nicknamed "Farting Lane"...
THE ALLEY THAT SMELLS OF FARTS!

- **Museums for all tastes**
Are you passionate about magic? No problem! There is the Magic Circle!
Are you crazy about comics? At the Cartoon Museum you will be spoiled for choice!

BRITISH MUSEUM

A day at the museum!

The *British Museum* is one of the largest and oldest museums in the world. Inside a building that resembles a gigantic Greek temple, there are over 8 million objects that tell the story of humans from the earliest civilizations, such as the mummy of *Gebelein*, affectionately called "Ginger" for his red hair.

• A great collector

Since childhood *Sir Hans Sloane*, British physician and naturalist, had a passion for unusual objects. His collection came to include over 70,000 items: coins, books, dried plants, and even manuscripts on bizarre animals. When he died in 1753, he left the entire collection to his country, which formed the basis of the *British Museum*!

DO YOU COLLECT ANYTHING?

• British Library

Not far from the museum, there is the National Library.
In addition to the ancient volumes housed in a striking six-story glass tower, the British Library holds copies of all books published in the UK!
To transport them to the reading room, a system of conveyor belts is used, similar to that in an airport!

LET'S DISCOVER THE MOST UNUSUAL STORIES OF THE MUSEUM!

• The dung beetle

(Room 63)

In the area dedicated to ancient Egypt, in the midst of mummies and pharaohs, there is a sculpture of a giant scarab.
This type of beetle is known for creating balls of dung that it rolls on the ground. In addition to eating the dung, the females also hide their eggs inside it.
For this, the scarab was considered sacred by the Egyptians, who believed it could be reborn after death.

• The Fishpool Hoard

(Room 40)

In 1966, some workers found a fabulous treasure buried in *Sherwood Forest*. It appears that the jewels and gold coins from 1237 had been hidden there during an escape over five centuries ago.

COULD A CERTAIN ROBIN HOOD HAVE BEEN INVOLVED?

• Hoa Hakananai'a, the moai of Easter Island

(Room 24)

It is over 6 feet tall and has pursed lips and an upward-pointing chin. What is it? *Hoa Hakananai'a* is one of the 1,000 moais of Easter Island.

THE SIGNIFICANCE OF THESE STRANGE SCULPTURES IS STILL A MYSTERY, BUT ACCORDING TO *RAPA NUI* MYTHOLOGY, IT APPEARS THAT THEY HAD THE POWER TO MOVE.

BE CAREFUL, YOU NEVER KNOW!

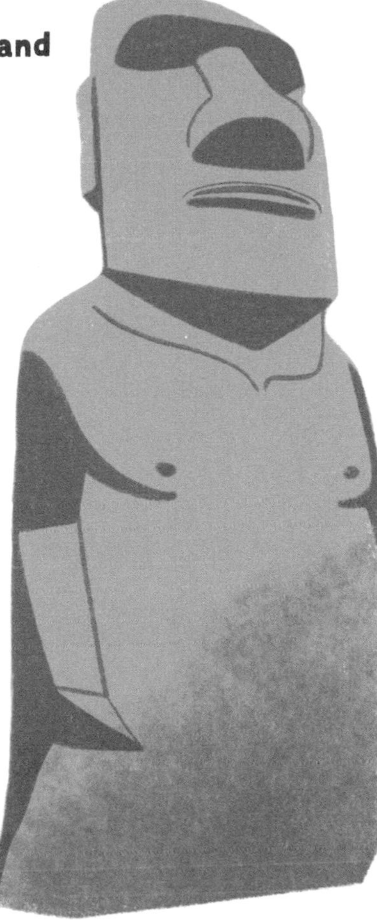

• The Armor Collection

(Room 93)

Samurais were ancient Japanese warriors. When fighting, they wore heavy armor made up of hundreds of small iron plates. Every part of their body had to be covered: from the feet to the head, on which stood a large helmet with a bizarre shape.

DOES IT REMIND YOU OF THE HELMET OF A CERTAIN *STAR WARS CHARACTER*?

COVENT GARDEN

Friends, I am a bit hungry. How about a snack?

The most important market in England was once held in the square of Covent Garden. Colorful stalls sold exotic fruits, vegetables, and foods; all around stood theaters and cafes. Today this area continues to be a lively neighborhood where street artists perform and art exhibitions and theater performances take place.

The ancient market is located inside a splendid building covered by a glass structure which, at Christmas, is lit up with thousands of lights. There are no longer only food stalls, but also craft shops, boutiques, and restaurants.

I SMELL FISH AND CHIPS...

• Fried fish and potatoes

Fish and chips is a much-loved dish of British cuisine. It consists of a large fillet of cod, fried in batter, sprinkled with salt and vinegar, and surrounded by delicious chips. There are over 10,000 fish and chips shops in England!

TRAFALGAR SQUARE

We have come to the most famous square in London!

The first thing you notice when arriving in Trafalgar Square is the column dedicated to Admiral Horatio Nelson.
The monument is in fact as tall as ten giraffes placed one on top of the other!

Four gigantic lions watch over the base of the column. To make them as realistic as possible, the sculptor asked the London Zoo to let him know as soon as a lion died, and when it happened, he had the body taken to his studio.
After a few days the smell had become unbearable and the artist had to finish the job without a "model."

• The one-armed hero
On the top of the column is the statue that commemorates Horatio Nelson, who died in the famous Battle of Trafalgar.

Observe it carefully: Do you notice anything strange?

YES, THE ADMIRAL WAS FAITHFULLY SCULPTED WITHOUT HIS RIGHT ARM, WHICH WAS LOST DURING A BATTLE IN THE CANARY ISLANDS.

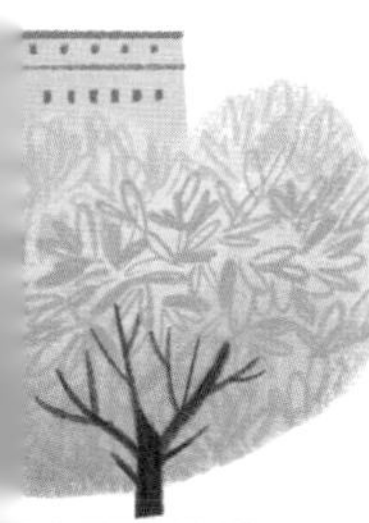

EVERYBODY ON BOARD!

• Double-decker bus

Once upon a time, Londoners used the omnibus, a carriage drawn by three horses that carried up to 18 passengers, to get around the city. In order to get off you just had to knock on the roof of the vehicle or prod the driver! With the invention of the engine, in 1956 came the Routemasters, the beloved red double-decker buses, which immediately became one of the most famous symbols of London.

UNTIL A FEW YEARS AGO, BUSES WERE EQUIPPED WITH A REAR PLATFORM THAT ALLOWED PASSENGERS TO GET ON AND OFF...ON THE GO!

UNDERGROUND

• The Tube

The London Underground started in 1863, making it the oldest subway system in the world! Each of the 11 lines is indicated by a different color, from brown to turquoise.

"MIND THE GAP" is the first thing you will hear on board, and it means that you have to pay attention to the space between the train and the platform.

• The Transport Museum

The most fun way to discover the world of public transportation is to visit the London Transport Museum. Inside there are over 80 vehicles—not only is it possible to climb on many of them, but young visitors can also pretend to be drivers, wearing period costumes.

Moreover, thanks to an interactive simulator, you can experience the thrill of driving a real subway!

Ready, steady, go! Let's start our last adventure!

ITINERARY 4

Today we will visit sights around the City of London, the historic financial district that alternates skyscrapers with charming medieval streets. We will peek under strange grates, we will discover the secrets of an ancient theater, and then we will move along the north bank of the Thames, where my home is!

So, come along and follow me!

- **Eerie but brilliant**

The much-loved red phone booth, one of London's symbols, was inspired by none other than...a grave!
Sir Giles Gilbert Scott, winner of the competition for the design project, copied the structure of a mausoleum seen in a cemetery.

3

TOWER OF LONDON

- **A more striking color**

Not everyone knows that the red pillarboxes, the famous British mailboxes, have not always been red. In 1859, green was their official color! After receiving numerous complaints about the difficulty of finding them, Royal Mail decided to use a more striking color.

IT TOOK 10 YEARS TO REPAINT THEM ALL!

GLOBE THEATRE

To be or not to be...excited about this? I am!

On the bank of the Thames is the reconstruction of one of the most famous theaters in the world. It was here that William Shakespeare—the famous playwright and poet, author of works such as *Hamlet*, *Romeo and Juliet*, and *The Tempest*—had his company perform.

The original theater was destroyed in 1613. The play being performed included the firing of cannonballs, but one of them hit the thatched roof, which instantly caught fire and burned down the entire wooden structure.

• Juliet...with a beard!
In Shakespeare's time, women were not allowed to perform. Female characters were played by male actors wearing costumes and makeup, who did their best to look like women...even with a beard!

• What's that strange boulder doing at 111 Cannon Street?
This large stone was allegedly brought to London by a descendant of the Trojan hero Aeneas, but there are those who think that it was instead part of the rock in which Excalibur, the legendary sword of King Arthur, was inserted!

"As long as the stone of fate is safe, London will thrive!"

That's how the legend goes, and whether it's true or not, better to keep it safe in a glass case!

LONDON SKYSCRAPERS

And now let's explore London from above!

In recent years, the city's skyline has changed in appearance. Alongside the classic silhouettes of Big Ben and Tower Bridge, there are a huge cheese grater, an immense cucumber, and a giant walkie-talkie. Oh no, my friends, I'm not crazy! These are simply the nicknames given to London's skyscrapers!

Nickname: Walkie-Talkie
Year of birth: 2014
Height: 524 feet (160 meters)
Number of floors: 37
Distinguishing feature:
Sky Garden on the top floor

Nickname: Cheese Grater
Year of birth: 2014
Height: 738 feet (225 meters)
Number of floors: 48
Distinguishing feature:
It is made up of 754,000 sq feet (70,000 sq meters) of glass.

- **Don't look down!**

Cleaning windows on skyscrapers is hardly a job for the faint-hearted! Brave cleaners have to rappel down the steep glass walls via a double rope hooked to the top of the building. It takes about 3 months for a team of 17 people to clean a building like The Shard, which is equal to the size of 8 football fields.

AND ONCE THEY ARE DONE, THEY HAVE TO START OVER!

The Shard

Nickname: The Shard
Year of birth: 2012
Height: 1,000 feet (309 meters)
Number of floors: 87
Distinguishing feature: From the top, you can enjoy the highest view of London.

Nickname: The Gherkin
Year of birth: 2004
Height: 590 feet (180 meters)
Number of floors: 41
Distinguishing feature: 7,429 glass panels.

Imagine your own skyscraper!

What nickname would you give it? How many floors would it have? What would you like to put inside? (For example, a basketball court, a toy shop, an ice-skating rink, Willy Wonka's chocolate factory.)

TOWER BRIDGE AND THE TOWER OF LONDON

Look! The bridge is rising!

Tower Bridge is another symbol of London. What makes it special, in addition to its two towers, is the mechanism that allows it to rise to let large boats through.

IT TAKES ONLY 90 SECONDS TO DO THIS!

IT'S TIME TO GO HOME!

Look over there! Do you see that fortress? That's where I live!
Since it was built 900 years ago, it has been a royal palace, an arsenal, and even a prison. Today it welcomes visitors who want to discover its secrets and admire the fabulous Crown Jewels.

• **Meet my friend**
According to a mysterious legend, if the ravens of the Tower of London die or fly away, the Crown, and Britain, will fall.
That's why my eight friends and I have a person who takes care of us. With his three good helpers, the Raven Master keeps our home clean, feeds us, and pampers us. In return, we must behave well.

Goodbye, my friends. Next time you come back to London, come and see me!

AND DON'T FORGET TO ALWAYS OBSERVE THE WORLD WITH EYES FULL OF WONDER!

LAURA RE

Born in Rome, Laura attended the Rome School of Comics, after which she collaborated with animation studios as a character designer, concept artist, and illustrator. After attending the International School of Illustration in Sàrmede, Italy, she moved to Milan to attend Mimaster's Master in Illustration. Here she deepened her knowledge of the publishing sector and the world of illustration for children.

DANIELA CELLI

Born in Florence in 1977, Daniela studied piano at the Luigi Cherubini Conservatory, after which she moved to New York and began studying criminology. In 1997, she returned to Italy, graduated in law, and obtained a diploma from the Academy of Dramatic Arts. Always passionate about travel, since 2008 she has been blogging about adventures with her family around the world.

White Star Kids™ is a trademark of White Star s.r.l.

Piazzale Luigi Cadorna, 6
20123 Milan, Italy
www.whitestar.it

Translation: Inga Sempel
Editing: Michele Suchomel-Casey

Second printing, February 2023

ISBN 978-88-544-1865-3
2 3 4 5 6   27 26 25 24 23

Printed and manufactured
in Slovenia by GRAFIKA SOCA D.O.O.

Sir Raven lives in the Tower of London with his friends. He is a very polite bird and croaks good morning to all the visitors of the fortress. He loves flying over the rooftops of the city singing songs from *Mary Poppins*, eating cheese sandwiches, and having tea with the queen.

Graphic layout
Valentina Figus